The Non-Sequitur of Snow

The Non-Sequitur of Snow

Shari Kocher

PUNCHER & WATTMANN

First published in 2015

Published by Puncher and Wattmann
PO Box 441
Glebe NSW 2037

http://www.puncherandwattmann.com
puncherandwattmann@bigpond.com

National Library of Australia
Cataloguing-in-Publication entry:

Kocher, Shari

The Non-Sequitur of Snow

ISBN   9781922186829

I. Title.

A821.3

Cover design by Matthew Holt

Printed by McPherson's Printing Group

This project has been assisted by the Australian Government through the Australia Council, its arts funding and advisory body.

Australian Government

Australia Council
for the Arts

for Theresa Mary
and for Janine Sarah

Contents

it is easy to forget
what I came for
among so many who have always
lived here
swaying their crenellated fans
between the reefs
and besides
you breathe differently down here

Adrienne Rich

A white flower grows in quietness.
Let your tongue become that flower.

Rumi

,

Snowmelt

So then let the Mountain be.
Let the hush of apples and ladders be as they are.
Let the shoes empty that enter the traffic
and release from its flow
the hush of a halo. Let the hush be
a halo. Let there be mourning any time of the day.
Let there be tears and fish in the sky
and on the trams and in the houses
the lips and hands of the powerful purpose
hungry for hush, and starving.

Let rain in a cup be. Let the hour.
Let the grace of a face immersed in hush
be the grace of a face immersed in hush.
Let the stars, the sun, the enraged flowers
not burning bodies of gas that shine
but Song be let Song be the hush divine.

The Non-Sequitur of Snow

once upon a time on a Sunday
       since ladders go up and down
       because like snow the frangipani was falling

a solidified tear stood in a ducted doorway
       what is the shape of a note in the dark?
       once upon a time on a Sunday

she looked up and the sky was the flattest blue
       there was no talking or if there was talking it was
       the eyelash running along a parallel hallway

since time unloads its palmings
       since spiders curl up
       in corners not of their own making

what is the smile of a small evil
       bouncing off the unwanted light
       in a darkened room of doorways

what is its scale?
       since she imagines clouds taste like frangipani
       flying forward not backward to the rolling

open of a stone that tasted once
       of honey and salt and the unpeeling
       of figs on a tongue made for singing

no prayer but that which exists
        in a mouth on a breast by a river
        built on the fruit of all her soul's doorways

smooth as a wish in the hand
        since ladders climb both ways
        and darkness is water

your soul quivered once
        like mine against a blue wall maybe
        still standing in the bluest dark

the curve of her own imminent horizon
        horizonless and humming what if
        the train was full

the clouds were heavy
        she arrived early and
        it began to snow

The train was full

shoes were sprouting ears
legs running without bodies without feet
a bell dug from mud and water
impaled on a boat sailing with arrows after it
bent figures whose torsos fit the shape of keys
the knife with the mould on it
my dress with the hem hanging

hands scrubbed raw the pluck of feathers
all the fruit rotting
the weatherboard splinters
the mad bearded potatoes
glowing in the ground
beget beget beget
war coming down the driveway

the timber giants felled and falling
me in my loose dress caught on a flagpole
the flapping artillery in the blackboy clearing
sheets on the line heavy as thunder
faces ghost the breadknife
this spotted dress with the hem hanging
all the shredded skins

All the shredded skins

So when you step inside the circle,
what breathes fire in the cold?
Empty-handed, tableless,
how seize this sphere you cannot hold?
No apple glowing in the bowl,
how draw it burning to your lips?
Who are you here? What call
precedes you? What cry belongs?

Notes from the Abyss

(i)

The night you were made
the angels fled and everywhere
it hurt to breathe.

Inglorious descent
still trailing those clouds of glory-light
you cut along the blade that shifting night,

unmade in me
you rent the sky apart
and rearranged the stars.

(ii)

Am I an empty jug
all poured out
'jug jug jug / so rudely forc'd'

or are you really there
strange dumb bird
in a hollow nest

floating dense
as a star
inside an egg?

(iii)

When I was a child I was so scared

of the long dark downstairs toilet roaring
with the sound of frogs in the pipes and on the chain, some sitting
on the rim of the bowl, the world

tonight, this long dark wretched night,
rushes out of me from all directions
churning and croaking like a cistern full of toads.

(iv)

How to hold this pause of silence in a piece of music?
How to feel light exploding in your hand
when you're deaf and Vivaldi's *Gloria* rushes
through your fingers back up the waterfall

beyond the memory of your own conception?
For a moment I might have held that quiet
as a candle holds its lit canoe
afloat in a bowl of wax

but memory ruffles the reflection of its own benediction
leaving my body leaf-laden and bound to the death
of this slowly dying summer, while the ducks in their concrete pond
rudely carry on, regardless.

(v)

Polished floors, shiny walls, realms
within words within halls.

There but for the grace of God go I
   the woman beside me said
and looked away (not reaching
for my hand) there
     at the still point of the turning world

between the slanting rain outside
and a small cup of sky upturned in the gap of a broken blind
your presence encircled some other order of things

and I cried out
in recognition
without language
    turning there inside a trolley's wheels going past

the inconceivable
    inescapable
      knowledge of you

spinning out like a stone and falling
with an incandescent light
across the stirred-up sea-floor of my mind.

(vi)

Last night I dreamt you were a fish
slipping from my fingers so hard
to hold and I was frantic

trying to fly, treading air above
the heads and hands of people in the street
all snatching at my feet

when suddenly a dark line of men appeared
with black sails billowing in octopus ink
trawling the air with harpoons

and I flew
away, away with you
high above the city and its smear of lights

out, out toward the sea
the blue bright beckoning sea
and you were light again

no longer gasping at my breast
but breathing quietly
a shining silver thing

I could not comprehend.

(vii)

"Once upon a time

on a bridge, alone, in winter
above pine trees in grey mist
and purple birds whose cries

clung, glistening, to her woollen coat
your mother wept
and the sound of pine nuts cracking

burst in a shower of light
around you, and through the branches
a bright rush of birds with open wings ascending ..."

Take it as a gift, a sign.

(viii)

You move like a mountain in the sea
in me, a ripple, a wave, a whisper

and all the fish in my closed arc of heaven
stop swimming
as your tiny hand unclasps

a pearl and floats
palm upwards like a starfish in the night.

(ix)

Nothing in this white room's glare
is visible as it really is.

Here is the garden
we did not enter:
you could be anyone.   Let's start
again.   You're someone from long ago
I haven't met yet
though you seem to know me well enough.

Here   take my shawl
of bone   it's lace   finely spun
runs in the family I suppose
but warm and you'll need it
out there in the garden:
the ivy on the wall
resists all light.
          Don't expect
roses
     but there'll be music of a kind.
Listen: the night air's loud with it already
frogs singing somewhere,
hidden, close to water.
No doubt
you're planning fireworks
          you're good at turning darkness
          inside out
just go easy:
          your exit's bound to startle
          these ever thinning walls.

*

You speak   and your voice
becomes your feet making butterflies
under my heart   if only
    you could hold me close
    this searing night
        which breaks apart again against
    the weight and hate of how
    you came to be

        but I am elsewhere
inside this cone of light
crowning at the window
        where a bird calls

high above the sea
    insistent as salt
rushing out of me in one slick wave
thrumming like thunder

your voice
    a shell-sharp cry
thumps against my ribcage
    and pummels me with joy.

*

Beyond the garden
there's a quiet gathering
of light, of feathers, of waters rippling
backwards
        outwards
dimming the noisy world.
I am here
        you whisper.
                We have arrived.
                        You'll find the music changed …

The Music

i.m. Joan Irene Burgess Rodoreda

well   i did ask that you let me return as a daisy
so i guess it's only fitting   thank god for small mercies
not in a jam jar   so here i am

nothing fancy but enough to see by
the whole of my body the sun rotating my daily sky
and with it the thrum of the bee rasping and grasping

the honey from me   nothing much has changed i guess
but in the moonlight when the moths come
i curl up, an eyelash, close myself to

their pale bodies resting on me
the weight of the dream of my own mute feet
deep in clay and dying to be free

Clay

clay feet   clay head   clay heavy
like lead   like the frown of a clown
my small son's head   lit from behind
like an angel she said   but he is not
an angel   though he is closer
to one than some   though he is making one
for the nativity table   though he is frowning
why is he   frowning   his hands
deep in the puzzling clay
why do   his angel's wings
keep falling off   keep falling
off the nativity table   and   *How do you get a halo to stick*
above a clay head?   he wants to know
How do you make it ... hover?
and then of course there is my mother
who hasn't visited in years but
here she is   frowning my son's
frown as her fingers roll out
a hoop as large as a boot
for the halo she droops over my son's
angel's arm   and he is pleased
with this halo doffed like a hat
or like the boomerang that bounces
back   and my mother is pleased
to watch the clay grow under his hands
the same clumpy feet
we all know belong to the friend called Hugo
who arrived one night in top hat and gumboots
to live under the bed   *That's right*

she says and tilts my son's head
(his shining head)   to plant a kiss that began
long ago in the top left-hand
corner of the window   now framing
her face   the bones of her face
her fine dry hair on fire

Spoons

crowded in drawers or leaning
precariously by the sink
their metal mouths
pursed and shrinking
the way my mother shrank from us
as if each child that swelled inside her
gouged her out a little more

until we became mouth
by mouth a set of spoons
unpolished mostly bent
but for the one
sterling silver boy
who would save us take us all
away to some shining place

someday or so I saw
and blindly hungered for
in that swift brief look of love
she reserved for him
which seemed to linger in a space of light
framed by the door where he had stood
or the kitchen window his hair alight

his toast encrusted knife
plunged handle-up in the butter dish
the lemons on the tree outside
vivid against the foliage hardly stirring
the way she looked at him
the pause of her spoon
and her mouth

Breakfast at Full Tide

after the painting of the same title by Kerry Johns

Breakfast at full tide beneath a darkening sky.
The table rocks the bright sea-bed, a boat.
Children, minnows darting, anchor the yolk,
laced in salt and pepper, this swimming egg that lies
like the morning, its veins undone before the day begun,
the rim of your cup ablaze. Why *must* you be hurrying,
still wet from the shower, out the door? This billowing
tide enclosed, awash with dishes and dirty sun-
light, flooding the walls with mashed banana,
something slips; I'm in the thick of it; pulls asunder.
What's the matter? The backwash of the day's hard clatter
split wide open. My legs that drip with seed like lava.
No good morning. The chairs accuse. The children fight.
I squint and bump my bones on too much glancing light.

Bellbird Gully

after Eugene's Falls, *by A. Frances Johnson*

inside the invisible atlas of a wave
possessor of savage kindness   two-tenths of the way
the rock wall of self   splits the unbound gaze
into a spume of wonder   the terror and fascination
of a pencilled hand stencilling in lead
the intricacy of water   that immutable
breadth and depth   approaching the very *whatness* of things

grown obdurate   skin-cells stretched
in vague permutations of sky
the sideways lurch of the mind   that can never
know itself   that beguiling
illusion of cognition   that atomised
density of world
who can breathe   grown thin and stretched

on the breath of forgetting
what once   you will never scale
that rock face of wall   the nature
of nature   grown impossibly   immense
no scale can map   the implausible plosives
of a future city   scant as cloth
fungal-flowered mildewed mosquito-mangy

progressively receding   the impression of distance
a mirage   a horizon
managed best   when drawn
      with dynamite
that alluvial blast of time   reductive
as recompense   the doubting
earth   denied

Flow, Repetition, Decay

rain in the night
a soft green world
the clicking of frogs and crickets
the man beside me deep in his swamp

        a soft green world
        burning songs in the darkness
        the man in the photograph deep in his swamp
        creaking his qualities like timber

songs that burn in the pitted darkness
lines of ibis that curve and spool
his shining qualities that creak like timber
a parachute billowing silkily down

        lines of ibis that curve and spool
        a soft green darkness lit with spears
        a parachute billowing silkily down
        sluicing the moss on the bridge with erosion

a soft green darkness lit with spears
we reach and sink knee deep in grass
sluicing the moss on the bridge with erosion
the gloss of a spider a delicate crystal

        we reach and sink knee deep in grass
        fiercely enfolding the silk inside
        the spider's belly glossed in crystal
        clicking with the song of a cricket

Strawberries

Do you remember that poem you liked so much
you put it in your back pocket and carried it around for days
close to your cheek as you used to say
till it went through the wash and came out like confetti
all through our clothes?

It had strawberries in it, and a bucket with a proverbial boy
and girl moving along a row which is why
I thought you liked it since you proposed that day
even though you say you thought it was later
you can't remember

the mud seeping into the knees of your jeans
and I can't remember what exactly I said
but I know it was *yes* and you went on filling your bucket
so quietly and the strawberries came away in your hands
so easily you didn't drop or bruise a single one

and all the while your eyes held the sky and looked on me
taking my bucket when we were done so tenderly
I thought my heart would burst at the red mound of fruit
you weighed and paid for
the silver scales flashing in the sun

and I sat with the tray on my lap in the car, the scent
of strawberries in my hair, everywhere, certain
I would remember every minute of that day, the light
on the hill glancing off the dashboard in golden
wristbands, your every hair illuminated

I could have wept, and yet I don't remember
what we said or how we came together so ordinarily
we don't even have a story
how we met, and when people ask I'm always
a little embarrassed (given you're so exotic around here)

so I tell them I wanted your bike and you wouldn't
sell it to me which isn't at all how it was
but I don't tell them how you sold it afterwards
to someone else and bought a racer with a crossbar
I couldn't ride

or how you held my baby, three days stubble on your chin
and proposed again
the morning light knocking my heart open
even though I'd already said yes and it was nobody's
business why you cried

and I was too stunned and lost
(you called it grace)
to wipe your tears away.
How could you not, now you say
you don't remember that strawberry day?

'Cannibals at Dinner in Formal Attire'

said the clown with the crooked teeth
sitting silent at a table in black and white
shredded ropes still lift her heart though the wind
tears it the waterlilies sing like ghosts

sitting silent at a table black and white
everyone talking moribund and mourning
the waterlilies sing like ghosts
crows cry terribly on almost bell-like notes

everyone talking moribund and mourning
bellies of pus make bundles of shining
crows cry terror on bell-like notes
the windows frame their blind intentions

bundles of pus make bellies of shining
tuna fin in the krill of their talk
the windows shade their blinding question
the cornflowers curl their astonishing tips

tuna fin in the krill of killing
a woman picks at the leaves on her plate
the cornflowers curl their astonished lips
while the shadows of birds pass over burnt mountain

she chews on leaves shredded with thorns
blankly believing in nothing
yet the shadows of birds pass over burnt mountain
and longing blows through her and burns her slow

blankly believing in nothing
she lies down in the night a shrouded blessing
longing burns her slow and burns her
breathing tears in the darkness an unsung flight

she lies down in the night a shrouded blessing
balsa flowers under the frame of her wing
breathing tears she names her hunger
there in the fold of a cloth draped over

there in the fold of a cloth draped over
the waterlilies sing like ghosts
moss grows outside on teeth and boulders
a chair pushed back in black and white

Dreaming in Auslan: a Study in Yellow and Grey

waking a little at a time the chain of light a helix at the window
    the way the night divides in ears of wheat
    a small low bleating on the edge of sleep
    that indistinct memory of sound in the heart
    of the ears that whither and fall silent
in circles that lap circling open

she will go the door swinging open to meet
    at the ends of her feet a spiral dream that small green
    frog leaping into hands in the darkness
    the rain a grey drum pouring the mountain out
    inside the belly of a cloud one hand on the cheek in a circle
is *grey* lit up like mist on the mountain grey face smiling

kissing a mouse *just as the raven of longing carries the flying frog*
    with blessings at the temple the bells on their bell-ropes
    in rippling circles denoting the density of *mountain*
    all alone yes her sloping feet carrying the baby with a pulse
    like a frog *a love-string stretching into the water*
the lit palms and lilting figures charging the ethereal body

with meaning the door opening on the fragrance of yellow
    the craziness of it! those curtains she hung like mustard
    barely a trace but suggestive in the circle that gesture
    by the temple hyacinths and lilies feeding
    on yellow cat's eyes twitching open
in the dream language a sleeping body makes in motion

loud as the hunt and the harvest moon dilated
     those eyes with the candles in them
     the pink cat tonsils and sour breath raking
     her chest imperious! demanding the night!
     the full gravital pull of the round white moon
eloquent as cat speech unfurled in a basket

the tenor a body makes in vibration
     colour of whale song quivering open
     sleeping a little at a time *the dugong grazes*
     at night on ambergris this raid on dreaming made
     visible in the pale light giving way to morning
woman with yellow sun on grey cat yawning

Cut

flying low under
  the pitch and tar
    the dream is drugged but time is
    the milky stem of a cut flower

        pulling up sharply
          through a sea of rock
            the urgent grasp of a hand
            in a blue glove grasping

land as the face-mask coming
  into view with the thumbs-up sign fades
    into a washed tenderness of stems
      night rolling in on wheels of sap

        soft faces cotton the touch
          of children strangers another hand
            holding a small cup of crushed ice
          that cool clear liquid drip

    breaking down
      the unmaking of a body's
   slipstream curling gold
the generosity of clouds

Canal Song

Louisa Bridge, County Kildare, Ireland

out walking along the canal
flat as the railway line beside it
rutted and teeming with litter
I see the limned reflection
of a leaf in water
floating above a face
stiff with pain
thinking about the russet
and gold and spiky fur
of the docks in the sun
the thistles bursting in soft
eiderdown flowers ringed
in barbs better than any fence
growing along a path
beside a canal with car bodies in it
a floating window-frame
the brimming light above the field
flashing like sheets of cut diamond
on the Intel factory windows
the rusted rim of a disused gate
and the polish of rain
on a rubbish bin
the willows on either side dipping
the whole weight of their lower branches
into the water and sipping
on the path by the river homewards
the underside of the leaf canopy
rocking like a boat
upside down in the sky

My Singing Empty Hands

I hold the boat steady and my sister
climbs in   the boat smells of lavender
as only the image of a boat
can smell of lavender in a dream

        water purling at the lip   my sister
        has not grown any older
        my sister says
        I smell of garlic

my sister takes the oars
you sit she says *I row don't you know*
anything?   my sister's words
smell strongly of washing powder

        she flinches when I touch her
        shut up she says *just let me row*
        my sister's hands on the oars
        smell of soap and some sinister

cheap perfume my daughter sometimes
wears when she is angry   my sister
closes her hands on the oars
my sister does not see me at all

        there's the smell of kelp in the water
        some rival in her head *do you remember*
        nothing she says *you say is true*
        I taste the snow in the air between us

my sister rows
precisely and with determination
the book grows soggy in her hand
ink   grass clippings   blood

> *why aren't you helping* she cries at last
> thrusting the oars at me as she sheds
> her crocodile tears *you never do anything*
> the book with which she has been rowing

from under her lashes my sister
watches me   my sister's tears
taste like lamingtons   my sister's voice
shines with the cut of scales

> my sister does not see through her crying
> the flash of real fish in the flashing water
> my sister sits in our small boat
> in the middle of that wide little water

with rounded shoulders
the smell of iron filings
something burning
she wears our mother's hair

Switch On Day

at The Royal Victorian Eye and Ear Hospital, Melbourne

Sounds like Hong Kong traffic
      high-rise birds and ribbons
            streaming out of your mouth

in flautist tones that taste
      like water—the green
            next higher note a thin

metal wire flensing
      a wolverine wind—
            speech is nonsense and I

am a sugar-glider reaching
      for the split sweet
            snake—a treble

note and its digital shell
      parting the curved air
            between the invisible

tree of your body
      its branches full of eyes //
            lumbering trams arrive

on threads of ting / a blank sky
      departs / cirrus clouds / drifting //
            Heavy as a swamp this morning

all I hear is mud—and you, Belovèd

     at your breakfast—slurping.

       Come, let's pull

on this suck and pucker—

     let's make Neanderthal footprints

       and speak in grunts and call this music!

Who cares what the world hears? This is Mud

     and You and I, Belovèd, are rolling in it.

       Glug-glug Glug-glug Glug-glug ...

A Letter to Dorothy Hewett

I'd always imagined
I'd meet you one day
nothing spectacular
just two women
going along the path
in a parallel world ...

It's winter in this room as I write
the sap pouring on the inside
of the closed-up leafless tree
tapping at the window
your book open
in my lap, and in my mind
that shining peninsular
with the garden gate
opening and closing continually ...

I suppose I took comfort
returning in the evening
to your poems, all those lamp-lit
hours with the house breathing in
and out the sighs of children
dreaming in the dark
knowing you were still alive
and writing somewhere
halfway up a mountain
with your cats and ghosts and armchairs
the way I imagined you, but not
in any detail

until the fact of your death
on the evening news
shattered the vase
with the dead flowers in it
spilling all over your book
lying where I'd left it
carelessly open on a chair ...

And if you were to return,
materialise in all your bulk and beauty
here on the sagging sofa beside me,
I would lay down my pen
and welcome you
perhaps like a daughter
and we wouldn't pretend
we didn't know each other
all the spirits rising
holding hands and walking out among
the living in the gritty light
all the stray cats and lonely footsteps—

(who is to say that scrawny
moth bitten thing with the hungry eyes
is not one of your tough little creatures
ragged and luminous as a street kid
hollowed out by morning
lying beside a garbage bin
in the first grey light of dawn?)

and the owl and the hawk with the broken wing
the ribs showing like whalebone caves
in the fallen architecture
the body gutted of all light—

who is to say that any of this
was meant to be?

I too prefer
to lie in bed and read old letters
shower late, watch the news
the world falling down around my ears
while I cook tea, switch to
a documentary
the kids tumbling noisily around me
arguing and snapping their fingers
and laughing, their eyes on who will get
the last potato—
but I am neither old nor dying
at least not yet
and have no excuse for the silence
your going evokes in me.

What am I doing?
What is this life asking?
The lunge in my heart
of lives crossing over
strangers no longer—
you asked the same questions
and lived and slept and raged
and loved and lost and raised
whole children, whole books
out of the ground
in ways I recognise.

Your poems
rally like phantoms round my bed
at night insomnia keeps me reading

cold pools of light thinking these things
and the towers keep falling
and the pages keep burning
in kerosene drums
rewriting the daylight

stripping me bare
they shout aloud
in tongues that flare
the skin around my bones
bidding me, as Lazarus was bid,
to get up and go outside
to keep on loving, and to live.

My Beautiful Fig Tree

split in half
at the base of its trunk
in a storm

fourteen years
into a marriage I had stopped
counting on

the rains came
breaking
the drought

and runners
shot up
everywhere

the following summer
my fig tree stood
tall as a shoulder

its furry umbrella
bulging
with purple fruit

come hold my heart
I said as you would
a fig so ripe

and sweet you don't
need to twist
for the gentle drop

of its giving
into your hand
but you let the fruit rot

and it was a feast of worms
for the shrieking birds
I fell in love with

who did not
and would not
stop their wings

nor fly
entirely
away

Swim

since ladders climb both ways   the shape of a note in the dark

frost on the grass   islands in the car park

water flowers   burn underfoot

no wind and no one else at the pool   liquid reams rippling

the roof beams behind her   as a duck's breast parts the cloud

inside a tree and sets the satin swaying   she parts and plunges with her breathing

last night's spirit passage   a bright mosaic floor

chest bone open to the bliss   driving the nameless underwater

the swim of this   the closest she will ever come to flying

struck like a bell dug from mud and water   the ephemeral two-toned note of her crying

drifts up on the out breath   its aerial touch

a drowned women's orchestra   buzzing the bones of her face

catacombs of tombings   she rises up to shower and dress

and because it must the mourning   Spring opens to greet her

glazing the asphalt   in all its burnings

the well from which   she turns to look

The Well

ripples its gauze
up and down the bodies of the bare trees
the scarlet sky the waist-high grass

swallowing water in the wind
who cares how her heart softens
the hard rind of a day lived without love

adjusting its sore gristle-gears to
the steady seepage of use
how well she could live without love

cool as a glass pool not too small a box
and calm but for this red gauze
rushing her through the gates of evening

massing and lifting its cockatoo cloud
its rip of rosellas bursting
its salted juice

a shiver of wings
gap-toothed and whistling
this stone on her tongue

The Canvas

Words became symbols, wrote themselves all over the grey-green walls.
Virginia Woolf

Dipping into the blues
and umbers the past
becomes a big old pocket
full of flint and shells
and one small book

speckled like a plover's egg taken out
against the silence and everything withheld
across the space of a small boat of a brush
reaching toward the hollow dwindling
of the next wave

Divided
between the fish writhing on the floor
(with a square cut out of its side for bait)
and the bright flashing of angles of thought
of a gull strung perpendicular to a mast in the sky

a woman must either
sit in that small boat in anguish too close beside him
or stand at some point in the hazy middle distance
with a voice or a brush or some uncharted sea
or dome of dazzling blue inside her

and create
even in the most casual assertion
an act of tangency

(contrary to what you might expect with all that body of water
lapping at the base of that proverbial island-rock et cetera)

and this becomes an exacting tedious business
(almost incongruous you might say)
in the face of that damned table upside down in a tree
(you would think it too precarious)
whose legs intersect the moving light of leaves

casting grey-green nets
across a man's mind
               his boots
                       his hands
clasped ridiculously behind his back

that uncompromising figure of a father
               (hers
                   mine
                     yours)
stumbling with empty arms down a blind hallway

one dark morning (or was it endless night?)
neat thumbs pressing the air out
of his daughter's throat
now sitting in the bottom of a boat
reading a book less than the size of his hand.

(The line jerks
another fish is caught
who can cut a perfect square?)

What does it all mean she asks
the tree   the boat

the middle of the picture
the hollow of the wave
all   all an insurmountable space

(what becomes of the remainder?)
every life a violent demand
and out of the aching blue
in a hand that trembles
the vision breaks up

the colours flap and tug
the canvas
unravels in the sky

The Scent, the Scent

my cousins' backyard fenceless and airy
the stippled brown grass hot underfoot
a sudden bindii patch   I drop
to the ground and smell in the blue
and green shade of the water tank the jasmine
of my wounded foot its honey and heat
and animal love bound up
in the whooping and yelling
of a whole troupe of cousins
not far off   there by the swaggering gum tree
calling me to climb to the top of the cubby
the splinters in the ladder   the ants
running over the sill the rope burning
as we slither up and down
between the woodchips and the resin
the green smell of moss on the hot granite
at the forbidden drop   sending the stones
one by one dizzily down
the damp earth growing damper the closer we crept
to the rotting mulch and leaf litter by the water
we called the sink with the earwigs scuttling
their sharp grey stink   back up the slope
to the smell of my own sweat my hands
turning the rose-scented soap grainy and pink
and brown in the sink   that heated-indoor smell
roast beef mint peas potatoes-in-butter
steaming the wax off the floor as we make our escape
from the table and slide on our backsides
up and down the hall   resin and jasmine in the wooden

blocks rubbing together and crashing around us
my cousin Paul whooping in a feathered headdress
and grinning so big!   and Julie rocking the doll
in its cradle smelling of moths and pears and tissue paper
me and Therese and Greg and Paul roaring around
(with Jen in her room and David hiding
my two little brothers somewhere about)
chasing and squealing and slicing the air
with imaginary whips till Mum says
settle down and it's somebody's birthday
jasmine round the table the smell of tree frogs
mould at the window   the red
horsehair sofa the downstairs
toilet on its rattling chain   all the adult voices rising
in a hubbub of beer and smoke and *out you go now*
the sharp poo smell emanating from the cistern
near my sand-pit that lonely green-slime-smell
on one side only of the perma-concrete blocks
stepping up and down playing in the grey sand
under the stairs with the silverfish
and the cane-toad croaking in a bucket
like a fat lump of poo   running out
into noon-time and the dizzy daylight
of my mother's skin the smell of cotton
growing on the line   burying my face
in the crease of her knees   her bare legs
hot beneath her dress in the sunlight
with just a hint of jasmine white and brown
the cotton of her skin
stippled scented and shining

The Bridge

i.m Darcey Iris Freeman, aged 4, January 29, 2009

First day of school and it's hot, hot, hot, and the traffic on the
        bridge
is moving too slowly. *It's fine, it's fine, we'll be on time!* but
        Dammit! he wants to belt
them. And the girl sucking her thumb and crying—*Stop that
        whining!*—hadn't he given
them the best weekend? Too much sun, yes, but he'd taken steps
with slip-slop-slap (she'll *have* to give him credit for that!) but
        no, just darkness, the water
below cold as her face and here in the car the simple disgrace of
        a daughter

sucking her thumb and crying for Mum—*Big girl now! C'mon!
        C'mon!*—this daughter
with the dewy eyes, the dead-spit look of that cold hard bitch
        stuck on a bridge
forever. *Because the judge said because she's the mother because
        the water*
without her a wrinkle a mirror, see how she likes it, reaching
        across, undoing the belt
No Daddy No limp as a doll always pretending see how she likes
        it, a few short steps
and Bingo she's over—*All-Over-Rover* like she's over *him*—
        what's not given

he'll not give back. See how *she* will cope with that. For what he's
        given
should be enough *should be should be* he has the right *His* sons
        His daughter

His by law and why should he share them, *angry women*
    everywhere taking steps
in court and out, England and back, and *still* she's not happy to
    see him—*London bridge*
is falling down—and she tumbles and fumbles as he clip-locks his
    belt
and pulls into traffic made lighter and brighter because of the
    girl high above water

airborne, her bones winging and singing the fear of her
    swimming high above water
the boy in the mirror white as a sheet—*Stop the car, Dad! Go
    back!* But no, what's given
you can't take back, his sons will learn it, the lesson today is not
    to belt
them but keep calm, in control, hands on the wheel, his daughter
behind him (an angel of blessing) Daddy's little helper glowing
    on the bridge
but he can't see her (*my God where is she? why here of all places?*)
    the Family Court steps

the glass, the guards, the marble echo, little boy Benji reciting
    their names. He steps
into darkness, the tide is arising, threatening to swallow, to cough
    him up, the water
is his daughter, swimming through her lungs, her back and tiny
    organs, the bridge
he crosses over—Leave him! She leaves him—Go to the girl and
    to the birth she was given,
to the woman who holds her crumpled and wet, go to the mother
    who holds her daughter
for the four crushed hours that are left. Go to every woman
    whose love and searing belt

of rage cannot save the girl on the bridge, nor keep the span of
      that seatbelt
locked across her lap. Given what men do, rage, rage against the
      steps
the dying of the light across the water, the murder of the night
      in every mother's daughter.

Blue Irises

blue tips on green spears
in a blue jug
beside a blue mountain
in the window far away

delicate spears like the tips
of the bare twigs
on the bare tree
beside the window collecting dew

green as hope
in a blue jug on a bare bench
beside a bowl of oranges
bright as scissors the future stems

Notes

'Snowmelt' responds to Rumi's poem 'Be melting snow'.
'Notes from the abyss' takes a line from T.S. Eliot's *The Waste Land* in part two and another in part five.
'Dreaming in Auslan: a study in yellow and grey': AUSLAN is Australian Sign Language. The poem quotes two lines from Rumi's parable poem 'The Force of Friendship'. See *The Essential Rumi*, Trans Coleman Barks, New Expanded Edition, HarperSanFrancisco, New York, 2004, p.84-85.

Acknowledgements

I would like to thank the editors of the following journals and magazines where some of these poems appeared for the first time, sometimes in slightly different forms: *Abridged 0-25: Silence, Best Australian Poems 2013, Blue Dog, Cordite, Crossing the Lino, Famous Reporter, Going Down Swinging, Island, Meanjin, Page Seventeen, Metabolism: Australian Poetry Members Anthology 2012, Overland, The Cows Were Here the Whole Time, SWAMP Writing.*

I would also like to acknowledge the judges of the *Page Seventeen* Short Story and Poetry Competition (2010), the Martha Richardson Memorial Prize (2010), John Masefield Poetry Prize (2010), *Writing the Forbidden* (2010), MPU International Poetry Competition (2011) and the UNE Literary Awards (2002) for honouring some of the poems in this book.

Heartfelt gratitude is owed to family and friends who have stuck by me these last two decades of life and love: especially, Andreas Kocher, Janine Campbell, Marcel Kocher, Theresa and Richard Campbell, Marianne Kocher, Maria Rodoreda, John and Ann Rodoreda, Peter and Pamela Rodoreda, Anna Simpson, Penny Drysdale, Nina Massarik, Leni Shilton and Wendy James. Affection and thanks also to Kevin Brophy for his earliest encouragement, to Ron Pretty and the Wollongong Poetry Foundation of twenty years ago for making those first tentative steps possible, and to A. Frances Johnson, whose formidable poetry continues to inspire. And to Jordie Albiston, Judith Beveridge, Yvette Holt, Jan Owen, Alex Skovron and Deb Westbury, for their many kindnesses, and for all the poems over the years: you have taught me gently and wisely, from afar.